Animal Homes

Contents	Page
River	2-3
Cave	4-5
Pond	6-7
Jungle	8-9
Snow and ice	10-11
Trees	12-13
Sea	14-15
Dolphins	16

written by Pam Holden

Who lives in that river?

river

Hippos and fish and crocodiles live in there.

Who has a home in that cave?

cave

Bats and spiders and bears live in there.

Who lives in that pond?

pond

Swans and frogs and ducks live there.

Who has a home in that jungle?

Monkeys and tigers and snakes live in there.

jungle

Who lives in the snow and ice?

10

Polar bears and penguins live in the snow and ice.

snow

Who has a home up in the trees?

trees

Squirrels and birds and opossums live up there.

Who lives in the sea?

Seals and whales and fish live in there.

sea

Dolphins live in the sea, too.
Splash!